oo as in m<u>oo</u>n

oo two dots above a word indicate plural

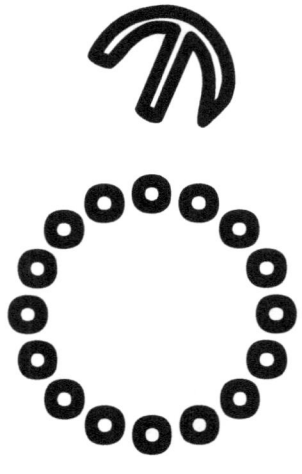

e (short) as in d<u>e</u>bt
ay (long) as in d<u>ay</u>

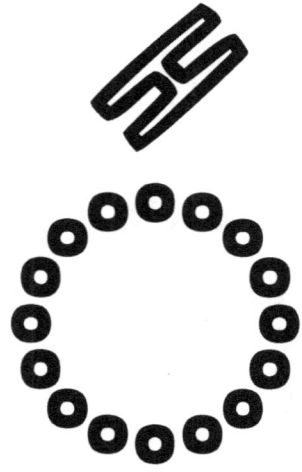

ee as in s<u>ee</u>

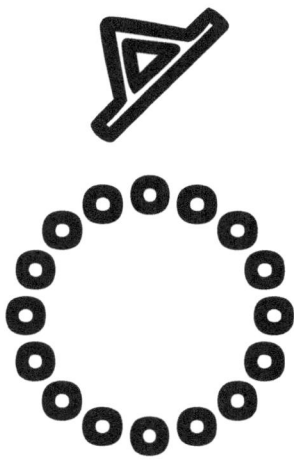

a as in p<u>a</u>t

o as in b<u>o</u>ne

Note. Vowels are optional in writing. When written, they appear above (or below) letters. For example, a vowel *a* above (or below) the letter *b* gives the sound *ba*.

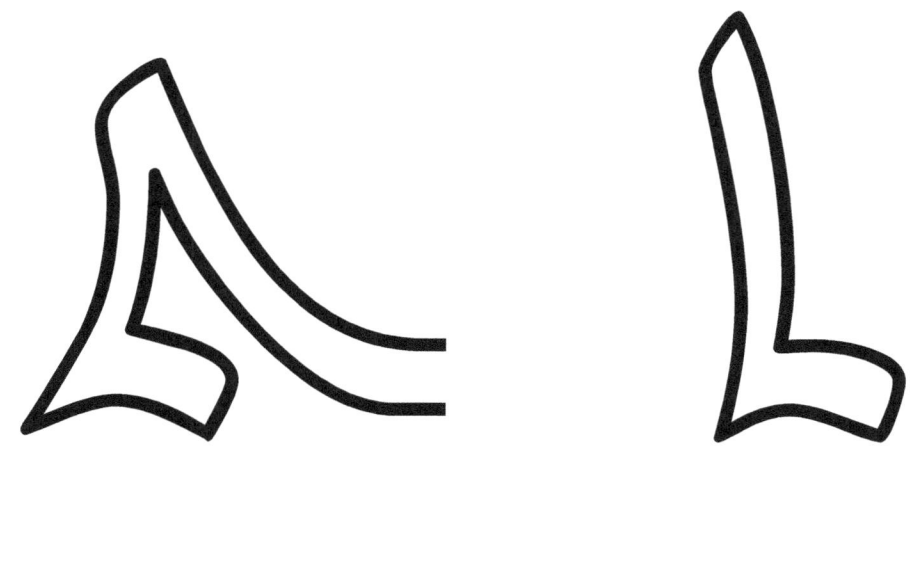

Letter Name	Sound		Word	Meaning
Taw	t		tur-to	cow

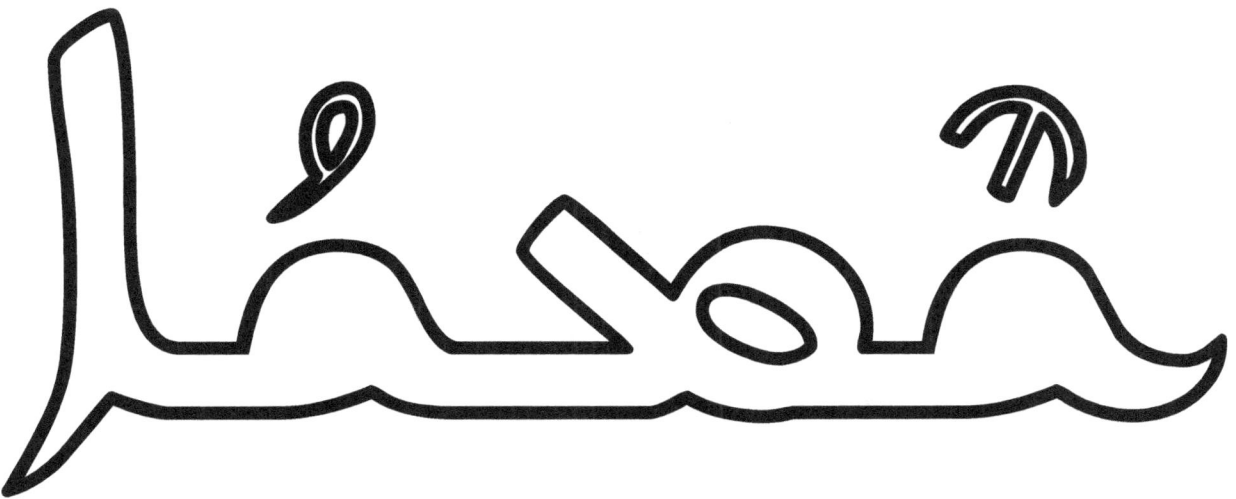

LETTER NAME	SOUND	WORD	MEANING
Shin	sh (as in shoe)	shem-sho	sun

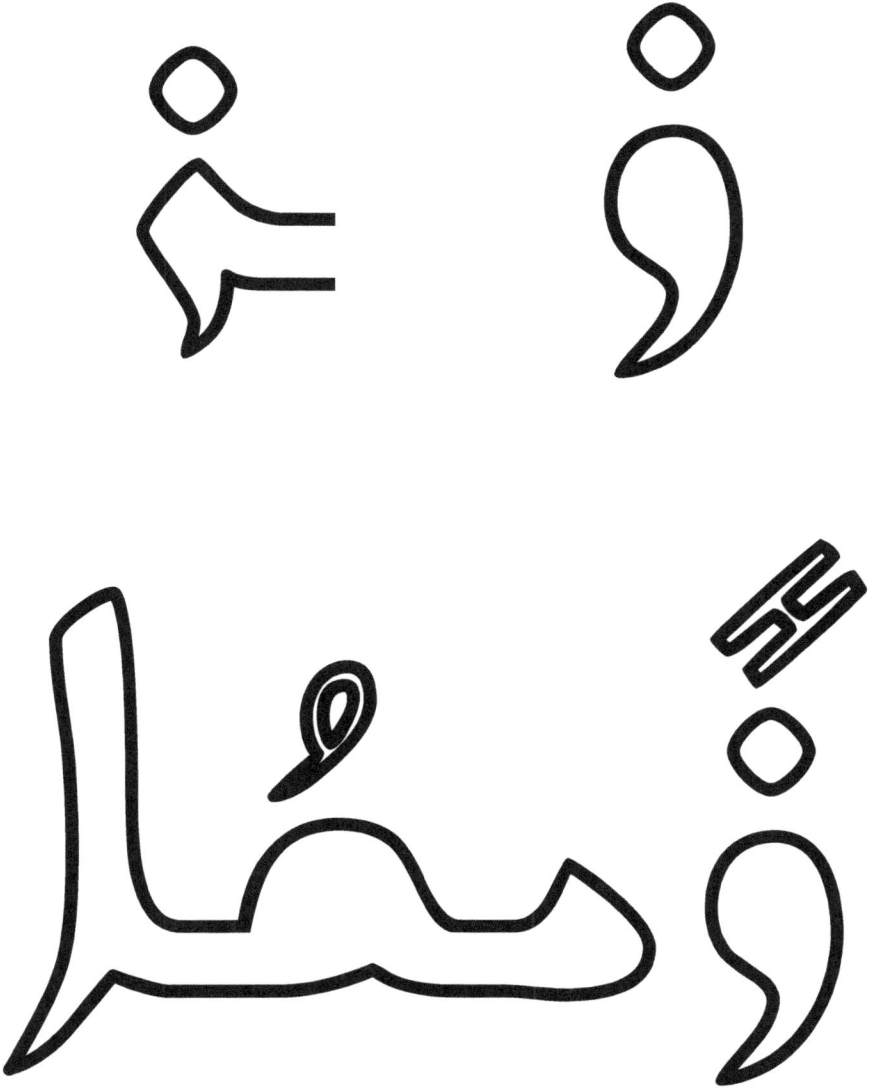

Letter Name	**Sound**	**Word**	**Meaning**
Rish	r (rolling r)	ree-sho	head

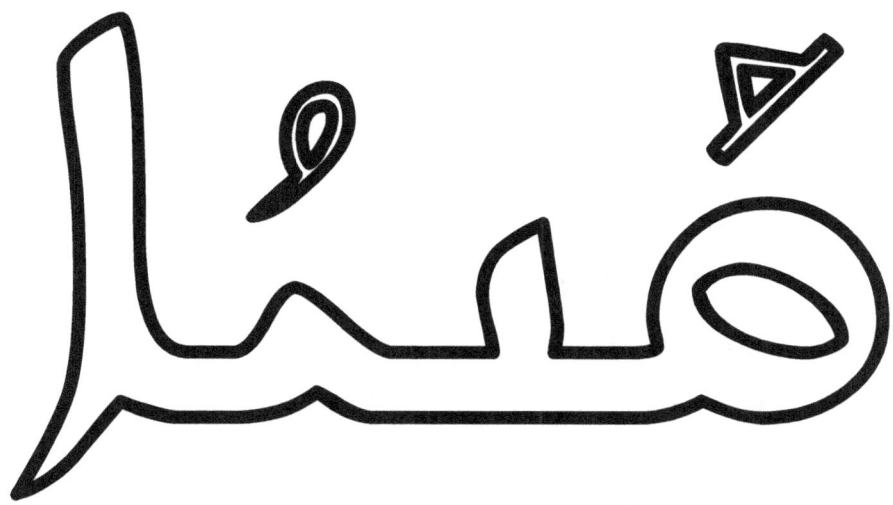

Letter Name	Sound	Word	Meaning
Qoph	q (gutteral)	qan-yo	pen

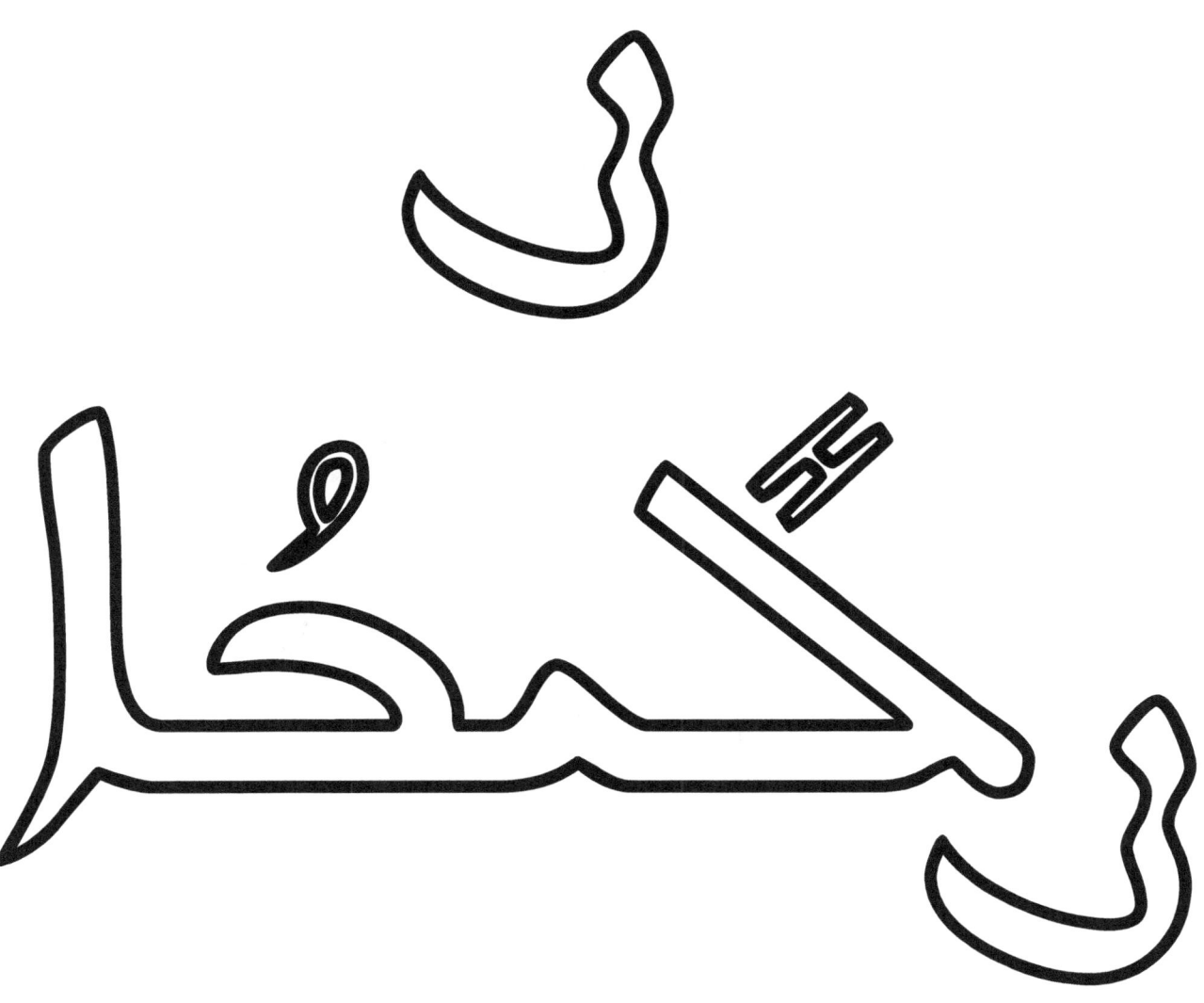

Letter Name	**Sound**	**Word**	**Meaning**
Ṣodhe	ṣ (emphatic s)	ṣ-lee-bo	Cross

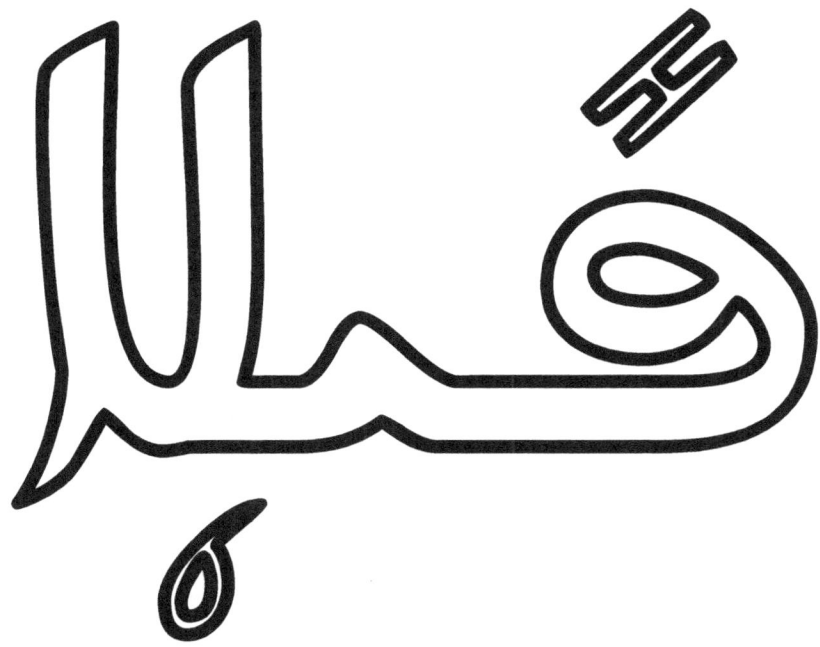

LETTER NAME	SOUND	WORD	MEANING
Phe	ph (f)	phee-lo	elephant

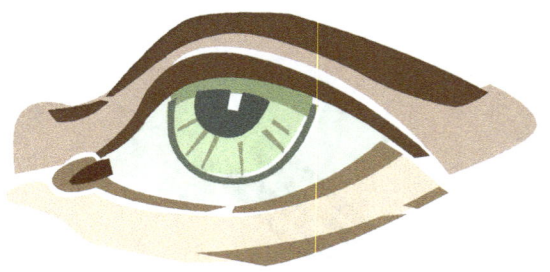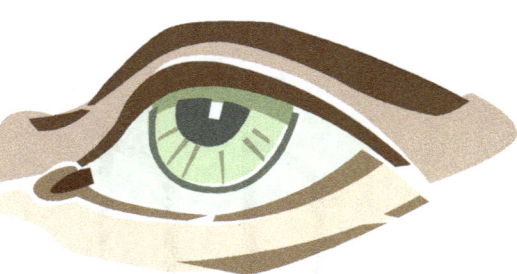

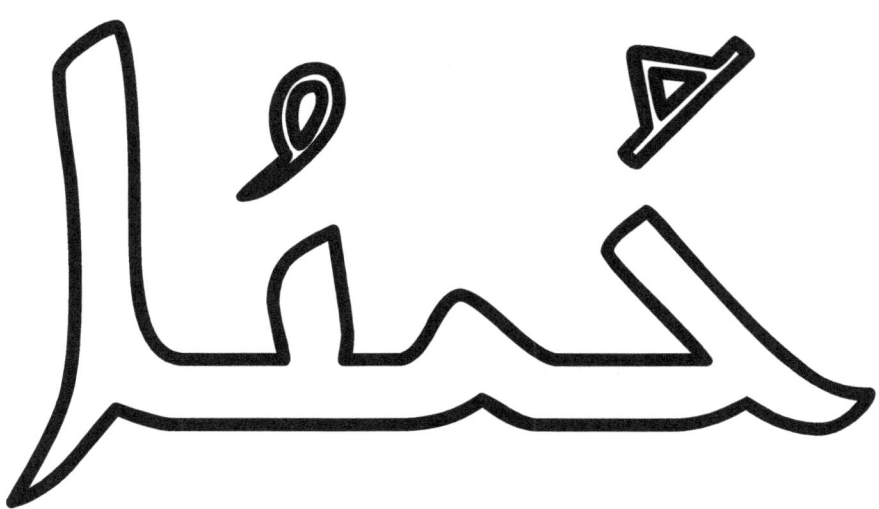

Letter Name	Sound	Word	Meaning
ʿE	ʿ (guttural)	ʿay-no	eye

Letter Name	Sound	Word	Meaning
Simkath	s	sah-ro	moon

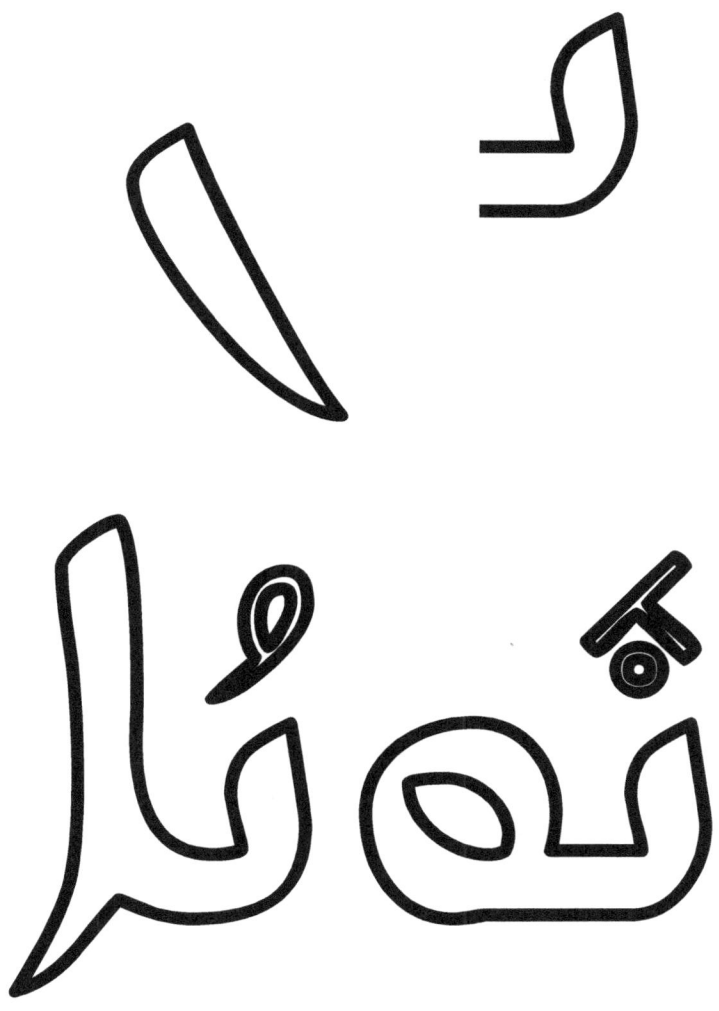

LETTER NAME	SOUND	WORD	MEANING
Nun	n	noo-no	fish

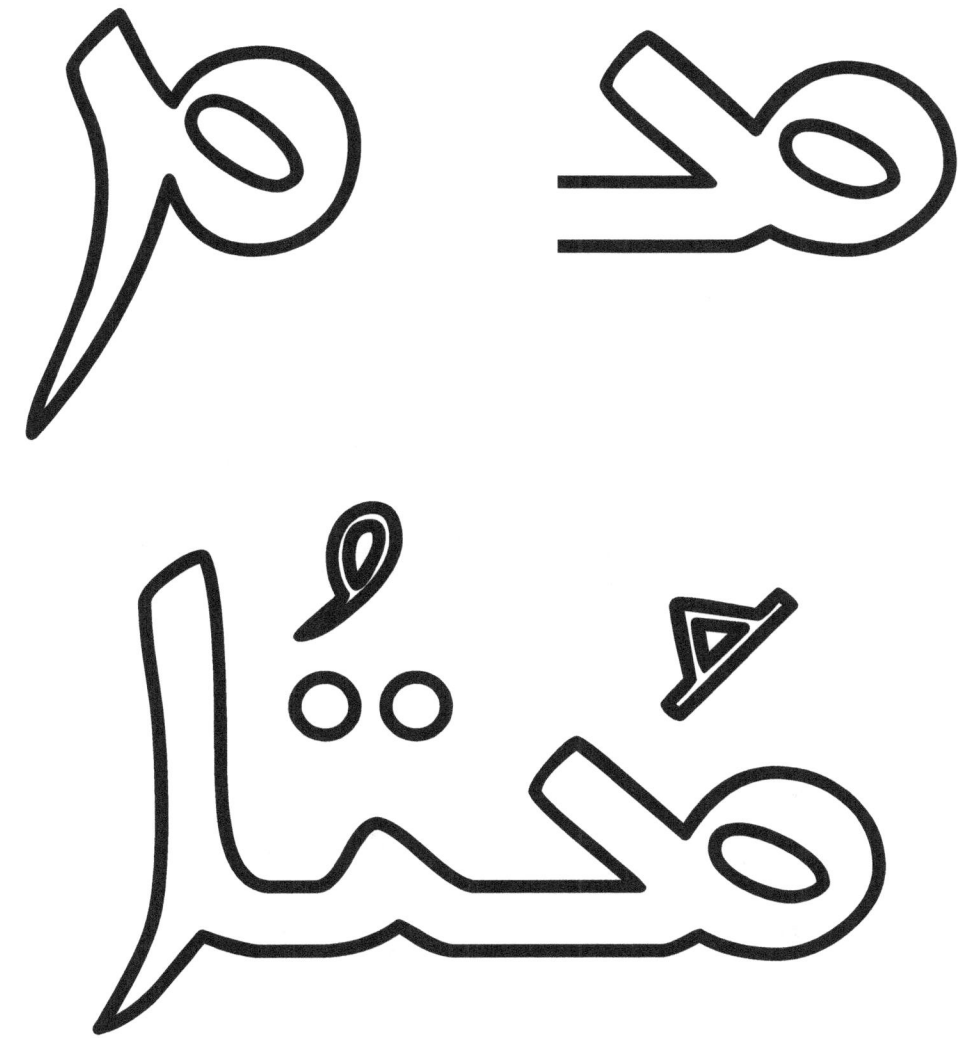

Letter Name	**Sound**	**Word**	**Meaning**
Mim	m	ma-yo	water

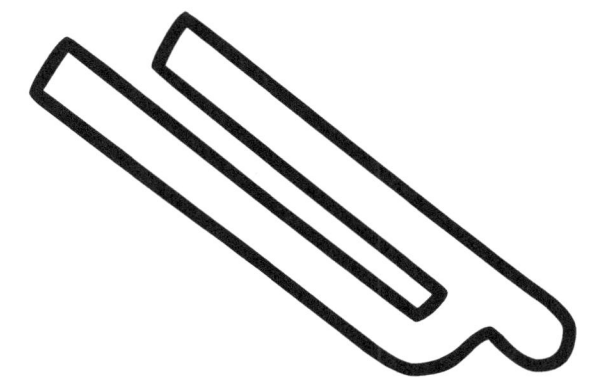

Letter Name	**Sound**	**Word**	**Meaning**
Lomadh	l	lé-bo	heart

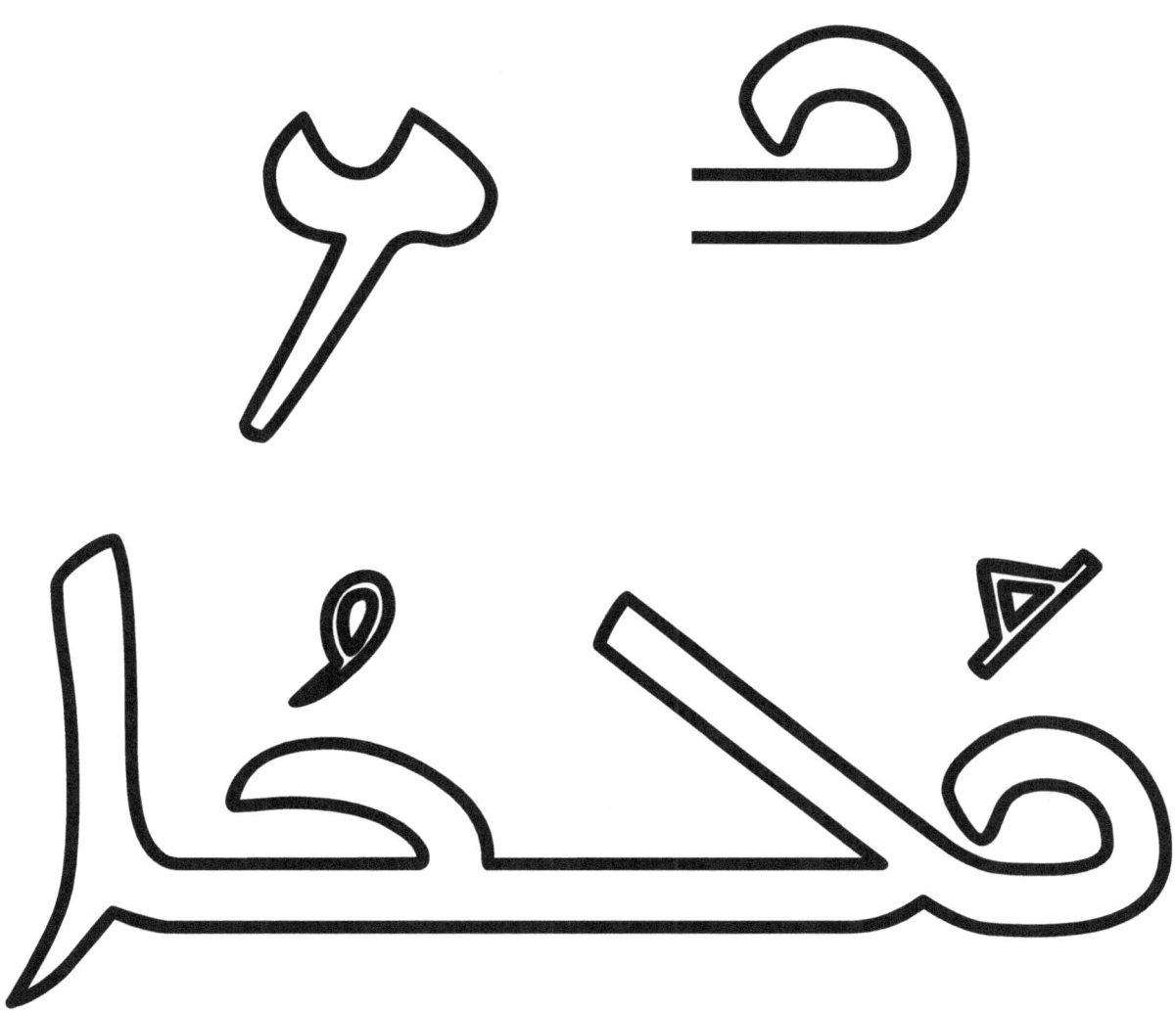

Letter Name	**Sound**	**Word**	**Meaning**
Koph	k	kal-bo	dog

Letter Name	Sound	Word	Meaning
Yudh	y	ya-mo	sea

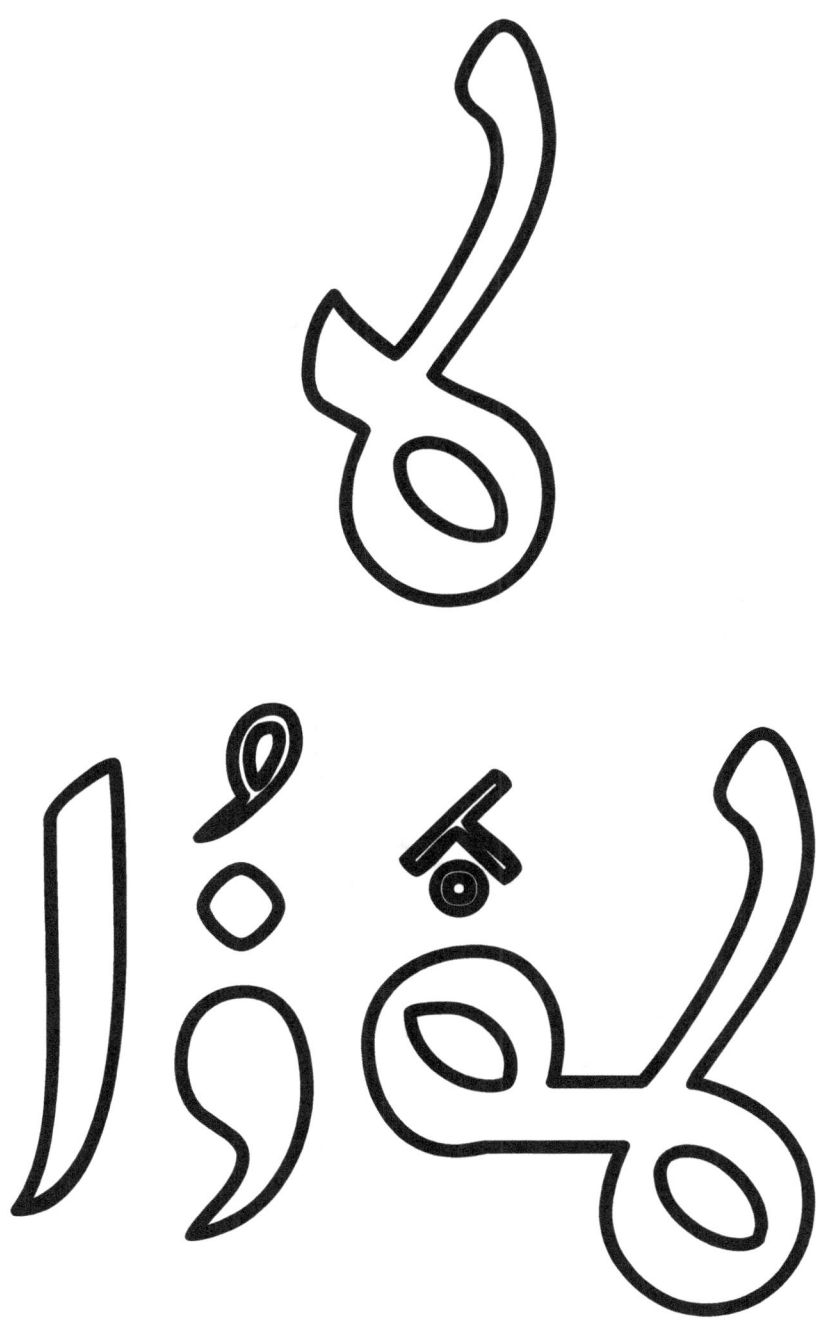

Letter Name	**Sound**	**Word**	**Meaning**
Ṭ	ṭ (emphatic t)	ṭoo-ro	mountain

Letter Name	Sound	Word	Meaning
Ḥeth	ḥ (emphatic h)	ḥal-bo	milk

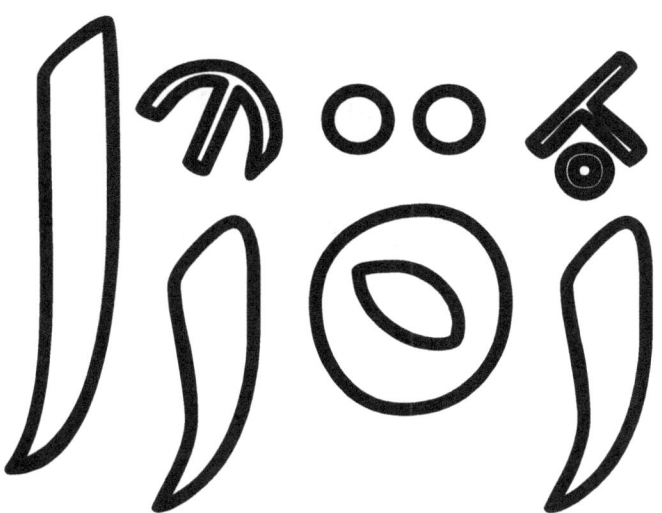

LETTER NAME	SOUND	WORD	MEANING
Zayn	z	zoo-zé	money
Note. Two dots above the word indicate plural.			

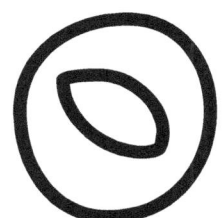

LETTER NAME	SOUND	WORD	MEANING
Waw	w	war-do	rose

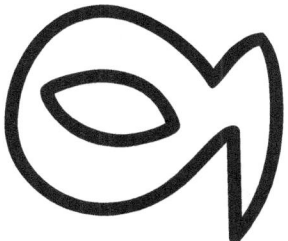

LETTER NAME	SOUND	WORD	MEANING
Hé	h	ha-bo-bo	flower

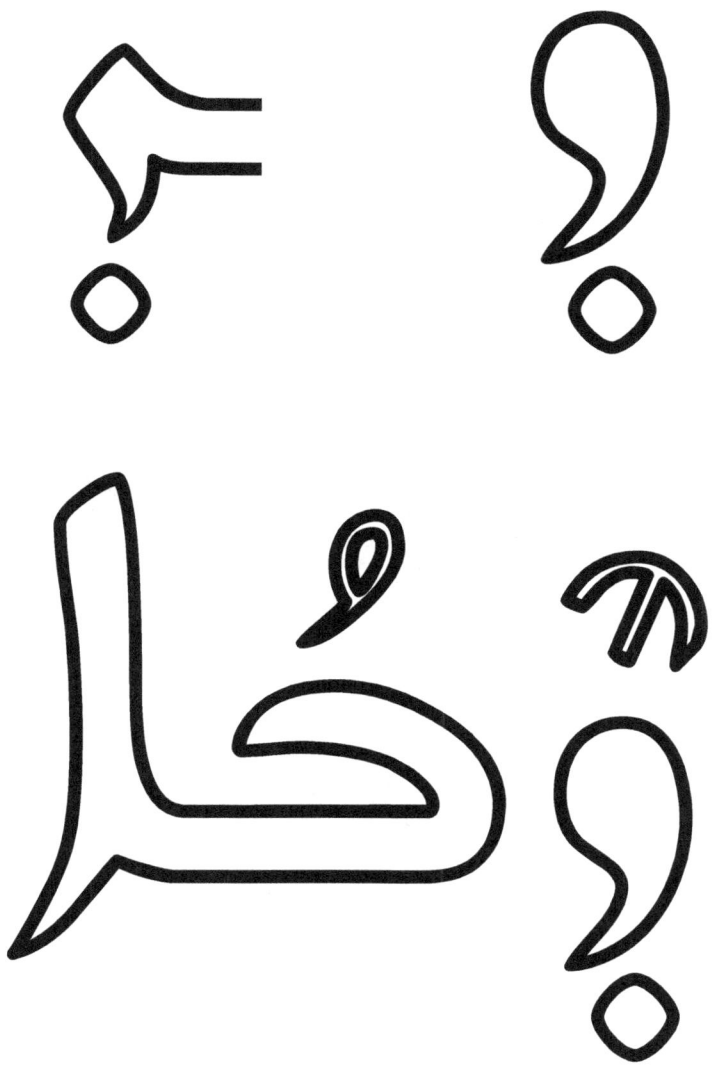

Letter Name	**Sound**	**Word**	**Meaning**
Dolath	d	dé-bo	bear

Letter Name	**Sound**	**Word**	**Meaning**
Gomal	g (as in goal)	gam-lo	camel

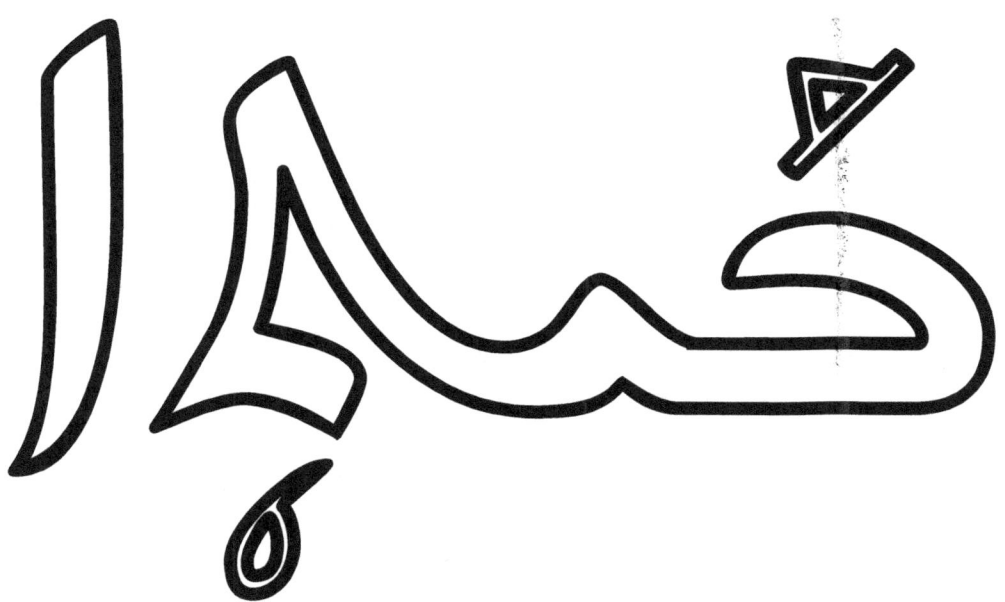

LETTER NAME	SOUND	WORD	MEANING
Beth	b	bay-to	house

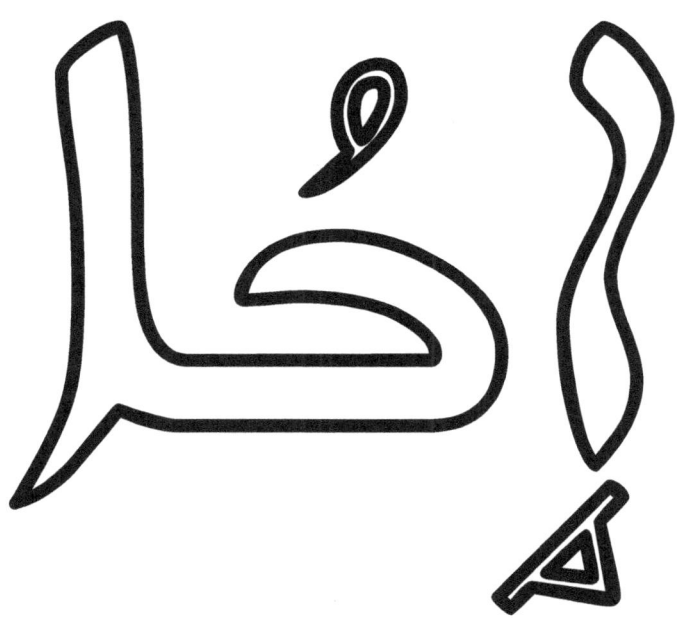

Letter Name	**Sound**	**Word**	**Meaning**
Olaph	(glottal stop)	a-bo	father

Preface

This booklet presents the Syriac alphabet according to the West Syriac script, known also as Serto. It can be used with children between the ages of two and six. Each pair of facing pages introduces a single letter of the alphabet with a word that begins with the letter in question on one side, and an illustration of that word on the other side. When a letter is shown in two forms, the first one (to the right) is used in the beginning and middle of a word, and the second one at the end of a word. The letters are hollow and can be filled and colored by children.

The boxed notes at the bottom of pages give the name of the letter on that page, how the letter sounds, a phonological transcription of the sample word, and the meaning of the word. Parents with no knowledge of Syriac can use this information to guide their children, and learn too!

Note that Syriac is written from right to left. While vowels are optional in the Syriac writing system, they are added here for the benefit of the parent, not the child. Children have an innate ability to learning and can be taught to read Syriac without vocalization from the start. Vowels are placed above (or below) letters. For example, if the vowel *a* appears above the letter *b* (e.g., ܒܰ), then one reads *ba*. The last three pages give a guide to vowel placement and pronunciation.

Piscataway, NJ

George A. Kiraz

Dedication

To

Tabetha Gabriella
&
Sebastian Kenoro

First Edition by Gorgias Press LLC, USA, 2004

Copyright © 2004 by Gorgias Press LLC.

All rights reserved under International and Pan-American Copyright Conventions. Published in the United States of America by Gorgias Press LLC, New Jersey.

ISBN 1-59333-112-6 (Paperback)

ISBN 1-59333-113-4 (Hardcover)

Available From:

GORGIAS PRESS
46 Orris Ave., Piscataway, NJ 08854 USA
www.gorgiaspress.com

Printed and bound in the United States of America.

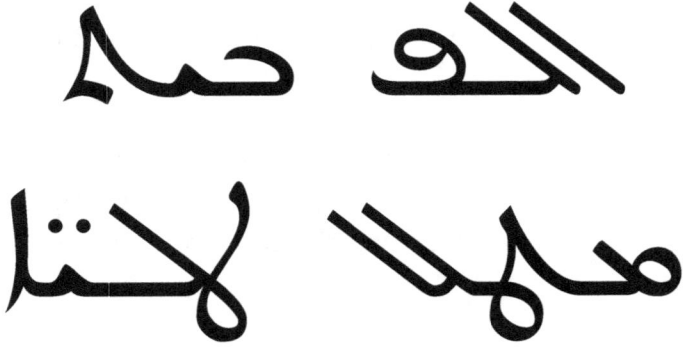

The Syriac Alphabet for Children

Serto Edition

By
George A. Kiraz

www.ingramcontent.com/pod-product-compliance
Lightning Source LLC
Chambersburg PA
CBHW080924180426
43192CB00040B/2677